The
WORLD'S
STUPIDEST
TWEETS

First published in Great Britain in 2022 by
Michael O'Mara Books Limited
9 Lion Yard
Tremadoc Road
London SW4 7NQ

A CIP catalogue record for this book is available
from the British Library.

Papers used by Michael O'Mara Books Limited are
natural, recyclable products made from wood grown
in sustainable forests. The manufacturing processes
conform to the environmental regulations of the
country of origin.

ISBN: 978-1-78929-492-7 in paperback print format
ISBN: 978-1-78929-493-4 in ebook format

1 2 3 4 5 6 7 8 9 10

Cover design by Ana Bjezancevic, using an
illustration from Shutterstock
Illustrations by Andrew Pinder

Printed and bound by CPI Group (UK) Ltd,
Croydon, CR0 4YY
www.mombooks.com

The
WORLD'S
STUPIDEST
TWEETS

Tim Collins

Michael O'Mara Books Limited

Introduction

It's easy to dismiss people on social media as stupid. You might get caught up in a raging argument with a stranger and feel the urge to call them 'dumb'. But hold off. Partly because the world would be a better a place if we all got along, but mostly because it does a disservice to actual dumb people.

There are people online so dense that it makes you wonder how they managed to switch on a phone or laptop in the first place. If you've ever wanted to know what it would be like to have a pet that talks, these people can help.

Don't believe me? Then check out these genuine tweets from the last decade or so. Just be warned that reading them will make your IQ plummet.

Welcome to dumb Twitter …

I swear someone needs to invent socks for hands, my hands are always cold.

♡ 5/5 stupid rating ○ ⟲ ☆

When you have the idea that's going to make you rich, but then you remember gloves.

 I jus wanna meet a female that can hold an enter lectual conversation with me

♡ 5/5 stupid rating ○ ⟲ ☆

Yep. Must be your intimidating intellect that's putting them off.

There is no 'I' in happyness

♡ 5/5 stupid rating   ⬭   ⇄   ☆

Unless you spell it right.

I went outside with my telescope and I couldn't find earth :/

♡ 5/5 stupid rating   ⬭   ⇄   ☆

Had the same thing when I went up the Eiffel Tower to try and see the Eiffel Tower.

Yes I'm vegan. Yes I eat meat.
We exist.

♡ 5/5 stupid rating

No you aren't. Yes you do.
The dumb levels here are so high I'm
no longer sure if anything really exists.

NEVER
GETTING MY
TONSILS REMOVED
EVER AGAIN

Everyone needs to get their tonsils and appendix clipped regularly. It's basic hygiene.

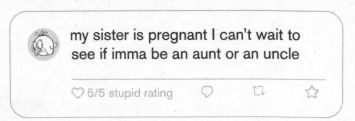

> my sister is pregnant I can't wait to see if imma be an aunt or an uncle
>
> ♡ 5/5 stupid rating

Not totally convinced that's how it works.

> OMG I just read that China is 12 hours ahead of America ... Why didn't they warn us about 9/11???
>
> ♡ 5/5 stupid rating

I know, right? And try getting the lottery numbers out of them.

Ima stay a virgin all my life. I want to set a good example for my kids.

♡ 5/5 stupid rating

Please don't have any.

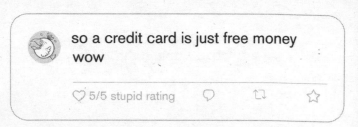

Yes, that's right. It's all free forever.
Give me some if you like.

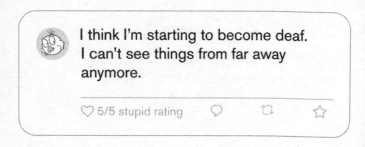

Then you'd be deaf and dumb.

I swallowed an ice cube yesterday and I haven't pooped it out yet. I'm really scared, you guys

♡ 5/5 stupid rating

I'd get it checked out at the hospital.
You know, that place you had the lobotomy.

 Why do women never have a DNA test to prove it's their child?

♡ 5/5 stupid rating

Someone wasn't paying attention in biology.

First Beyonce and Jay z in Paris then they in France ... Damn can't they stay one place for long.

♡ 5/5 stupid rating   💬   ↻   ☆

I bet they'll be in Europe next.

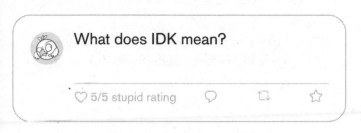

I hope this person has already asked hundreds of people, and they all said 'I don't know'.

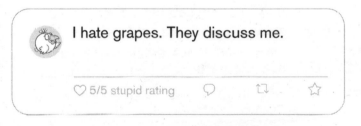

None of us like being talked about behind our backs.

I ran into a glass door and I think
I might have a Caucasian

♡ 5/5 stupid rating

If you were concussed,
you'd get words mixed up too.

 Nascar is nothing but a big scam to
get our hard earned money. They
never went to the moon. Every word
has been a lie.

♡ 5/5 stupid rating

I know, right? Do they seriously expect
us to believe someone could drive
a stock car to the moon?

Wow I can't believe Mount Rushmore was a natural phenomenon

♡ 5/5 stupid rating

The weird thing is that the heads appeared before any of them were president. They had to track down four guys who looked exactly like that.

 You just need to say good writtens to all the fake people in your life

♡ 5/5 stupid rating

I don't think this tweet is very good written.

I want my first
daughter to be a girl

*Something tells me your dream
could come true.*

Halloween falls on a Friday the 13th this year for the first time in 666 years. I'm totally stabbing someone.

♡ 5/5 stupid rating

The first part is not accurate. The second part might be, so I'm steering clear.

Don't y'all hate when teachers used to coffin skate your phone?

♡ 5/5 stupid rating 💬 ↺ ☆

Did they coffin skate all your textbooks too?

A kid born in 2010 is now 18 years.
Let that sink in.

♡ 5/5 stupid rating

*Someone was dumb enough to tweet
this in 2018. Let that sink in.*

how do i get youtube to come and film
me? i got tons of things to show to
the internet…

♡ 5/5 stupid rating

*They can fit you in next Tuesday between
a cat falling off a table and a baby biting
his brother's finger.*

We really shouldn't eat or wear animals. They are our friends. How would you like it if I ate you?

♡ 5/5 stupid rating

Needless to say, lots of men took her offer the wrong way.

 Atlanta spelled backwards is Atlanta. I never knew that.

♡ 5/5 stupid rating

I did. My cousin in Atnalta told me.

I love it when a hot guy passes by me and leaves his colon smell.

♡ 5/5 stupid rating

Did she mean 'cologne'? Or does she actually like it when men fart at her?

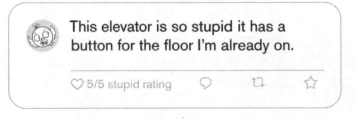

This elevator is so stupid it has a button for the floor I'm already on.

♡ 5/5 stupid rating

The one I'm in is so stupid it has a button for every floor I pass.

Lotto jackpot = $640 million.
Population of the U.S. = 300 million.
Let's just give everyone 2.13 million
and call it a day!

 ♡ 5/5 stupid rating ⃝ ⟲ ☆

*Does anyone want to check this calculation
before we celebrate the end of poverty?*

 Got a new number! Text me for the
number.

♡ 5/5 stupid rating ⃝   ☆

*Should I call round at your house
to get your address too?*

Do people not know have to spell milk? I keep seeing MLK everywhere. There's an I in there, people.

 5/5 stupid rating

I have a dream that dumb people stop tweeting.

Does is take 18 months for twins to be born? Or 9?

♡ 5/5 stupid rating

Let's just hope they're not going to be home-schooled.

 Idk what ima do for a workout tomorrow because the sun gave me a mind grain today.

♡ 5/5 stupid rating

Surprised your mind is big enough to fit a grain inside.

If the earth is flat do the moon and all the other planets are flat?

Yes they do. Don't let anyone tell you they didn't.

Jamaica a country in Africa right? What region they from?

♡ 5/5 stupid rating

Wrong, dumbass. It's in the west of India. That's why we say 'West Indies'.

 Don't understand why astronauts say they can't go to the sun because it's too hot. Just go at night then, doesn't take a genius.

♡ 5/5 stupid rating

Yeah, come on, it's not rocket science.

 Yall ever wonder if we're going to run out of gravity?

♡ 5/5 stupid rating   ☆

I think you'll be safe, given your density.

Will Smith kinda looks like the guy from fresh prince of bel air

♡ 5/5 stupid rating ⟲ ☆

And they say it's unrealistic that no one notices Superman and Clark Kent are the same person.

 Why do people die when they get killed!?!?!?!?!?

♡ 5/5 stupid rating ⟲ ☆

That's actually a myth. Many people survive getting killed and go on to live full lives.

A person who loves u will never kick you when your down or pour salad on your wounds.

♡ 5/5 stupid rating

It's especially upsetting when they offer to apply a dressing, then smother you in thousand island.

If a pregnant woman gives birth to two babies, if one comes out 11:58pm 31st December and the other comes out at 12:03am 1st January... are they still twins??

♡ 5/5 stupid rating

Yes, but only if they're Chinese, as they have a different new year.

Hope I done well in the English exam

♡ 5/5 stupid rating · ○ · ↻ · ☆

It's not looking good.

A fly just flew into my ear and I think it's eating my brain

♡ 5/5 stupid rating

I'm guessing that won't take long.

 If the goalkeeper is allowed to pick up the ball then why doesn't he just pick it up and run across the field to the other goal is he dumb

♡ 5/5 stupid rating

Shhh. I think you've just come up with a great way to win the World Cup, and I don't want other countries to know about it.

Boyfriend with no social media where you at?

♡ 5/5 stupid rating

This girl wants a partner who doesn't do social media, and has chosen to look for him ... on Twitter.

 Somebody born in 2020 will see the year 3000 when they're 80. That's wild.

♡ 5/5 stupid rating

This person either knows a lot about cryogenics or very little about maths.

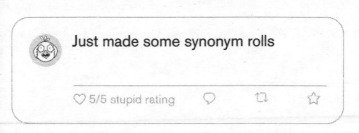

Just made some synonym rolls

♡ 5/5 stupid rating   💬   ↻   ☆

And some buns, swirls, desserts, pastries …

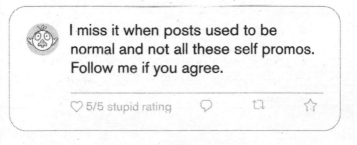

I miss it when posts used to be normal and not all these self promos. Follow me if you agree.

♡ 5/5 stupid rating   💬   ↻   ☆

But … but … that IS a self promo, isn't it?

Should I tell my parents I'm adopted?

Yes, but remember that it might come as a shock to them. Especially your mother, who went to all the effort of giving birth to you.

For all my followers with unproper grammar:
They're There Their
Too To Two
Your You're

♡ 5/5 stupid rating 💬 🔁 ☆

*Follow their example and you'll
never talk unproper again.*

 THE DEVIL HAS 5 LETTERS SO
DOES WEED IF YOU DONT THINK
WEED IS THE DEVIL YOU NEED
JESUS

♡ 5/5 stupid rating ·   ☆

*We can't smoke weed. You've already
had it all, by the looks of things.*

Completely lost my patients for the day

♡ 5/5 stupid rating   🗨   ↻   ☆

Let's hope this is a terrible speller and not a terrible doctor.

W.I.F.E = We In This Forever

♡ 5/5 stupid rating   🗨   ↻   ☆

No, that would be WITF. Almost the same as WTF, which is how I reacted to this tweet.

can your baby get pregnant if you have sex while pregnant?

♡ 5/5 stupid rating

Yes, and their baby can then get pregnant too. And their baby's baby. It's what Russian dolls are based on.

I Weighed myself today .. I'm 5ft 11

♡ 5/5 stupid rating

Same. But I'm trying to get down to my ideal height of 4ft 9.

you gotta have a cool car. you gotta have an educashion. if you don't have that then don't talk to me

♡ 5/5 stupid rating

If they did have an educashion, they probably wouldn't be a great match.

 was just trapped on the escalator for hours.....power went out!!!

♡ 5/5 stupid rating

This person better have meant 'elevator', because if they really stood on an escalator for hours when it stopped moving, there's no hope for any of us.

Microwave a penny for 1 minute and get a mini coin.

♡ 5/5 stupid rating   💬   🔁   ☆

And a free visit from a fire engine.

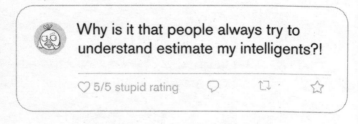

Why is it that people always try to understand estimate my intelligents?!

♡ 5/5 stupid rating   💬   🔁   ☆

Never understand estimate people. They might actually have quite a few intelligents.

If you smoke marinara, feel free to unfriend me.

♡ 5/5 stupid rating

I admit I've done Bolognese and Amatriciana, but I'd never touch Marinara.

Sometimes you gotta cheat on your girl to see if you really love her. If u feel guilty that means she's the one, if not quit playing on her bro

♡ 5/5 stupid rating   ☆

Yeah guys, stop messing your girls around and cheat on them right now.

Will.i.am spells William! Why have I only just noticed this?

Wait until they find out where Flo Rida comes from.

What country is the great wall of China in?

♡ 5/5 stupid rating   💬   ⟲   ☆

Dammit, I know this one. India?

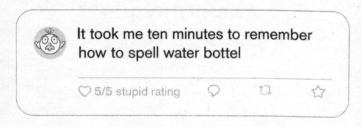

It took me ten minutes to remember how to spell water bottel

♡ 5/5 stupid rating   💬   ⟲   ☆

Ten minutes and counting …

Took the batteries out of the carbon monoxide alarm because the loud beeping was giving me a headache and made me sick and dizzy.

♡ 5/5 stupid rating   ☆

Weirdly, this was the last thing they ever tweeted.

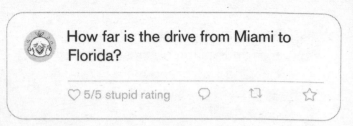

How far is the drive from Miami to Florida?

♡ 5/5 stupid rating

Anywhere from 0 seconds to 2 hours, depending on the part of Florida you're in.

My joints hurt really bad. I think I have Arthur Writes This!!!

♡ 5/5 stupid rating

You must really be in pain if Arthur had to write it for you.

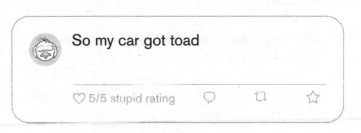

So my car got toad

♡ 5/5 stupid rating

Mine got Luigi. Let's race.

wake up eat poop school eat school poop running work work work eat poop sleep. << my next four days

♡ 5/5 stupid rating

And this is why we need commas.

Is pepperoni a meat or a vegetable?

♡ 5/5 stupid rating   💬   ↺   ☆

A vegetable. Like you.

Can planets be gay

5/5 stupid rating

Recent studies show that Jupiter and Saturn are flirting. We'll let you know if they take it any further.

My mom gon' tell me to drink more milk like bitch you know I lack toast and tolerance

5/5 stupid rating

Don't worry, there are plenty of products out there for people who lack toast. Toast, for example.

First time seeing the Specific Ocean !!!

♡ 5/5 stupid rating

Which ocean? You need to be more Pacific.

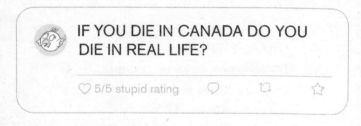

IF YOU DIE IN CANADA DO YOU DIE IN REAL LIFE?

♡ 5/5 stupid rating

No, but you have to go back to the
start of your current level.

I charged my iphone in the microwave now it doesn't work. What happened? HELP!!!

♡ 5/5 stupid rating

Are you sure you put it in for long enough?

I minus well get started on this homework I've been putting off.

♡ 5/5 stupid rating

Can't tell if it's English or Maths they haven't been learning.

its so hot… can we open the windows on this plane???

Nice to get some breeze and terrified passengers flying through the place.

You should watch the sunrise at least once a day.

♡ 5/5 stupid rating   ◯   ⇄   ☆

Is this person tweeting from a really fast private jet that lets them see more than one, or are they just dumb?

What kind of meat is lamb? Beef or pork?

♡ 5/5 stupid rating

If only there were some sort of clue in the name.

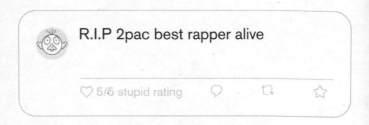

R.I.P 2pac best rapper alive

♡ 5/5 stupid rating

Can't work out if we need to break the bad news to this person or not.

 Is there a spell to become a mermaid that actually works?

♡ 5/5 stupid rating   ○ ⇄ ☆

Contact between humans and merpeople is strictly forbidden. Go no further down this foolish path.

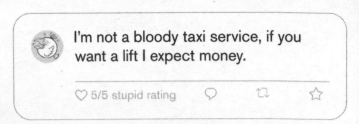

I'm not a bloody taxi service, if you want a lift I expect money.

♡ 5/5 stupid rating

But ... that's exactly what a taxi service is.

Aye serious question ... How can deaf people read?

♡ 5/5 stupid rating

*They get their blind friends to read
things out for them.*

My son does not like chicken. I think he might be a vetinarian.

♡ 5/5 stupid rating 💬 ↻ ☆

Why? Does he keep trying to revive it?

If youre anorexic just eat lol

♡ 5/5 stupid rating 💬 ↻ ☆

This person has great advice. If you're clinically depressed, just cheer up lol. If you're blind just see lol.

Tampons should not be free, why does everyone keep saying they should be?? if u can't control your bladder then that's not taxpayer's problem!

♡ 5/5 stupid rating

Maybe a little more of that tax should be spent on education.

guys I just realized finding nemo is called finding nemo because they're trying to find nemo

♡ 5/5 stupid rating

I really hope this person explains the title of Snakes on a Plane next.

 Do french people think in french or english?

♡ 5/5 stupid rating

They think in English like everyone else in the world. It's weird how they translate it into another language before they speak, though. You'd think it would be easier not to.

 I hate it when people act like they're in love with their newborn baby when they just met it 2 minutes ago

♡ 5/5 stupid rating

Exactly. Don't rush into things. Take the time to decide whether you like your baby or not before bringing it home.

Omg as if I have just found out that pirates are acsually real

I hope you didn't find this out while captaining a cargo ship around the coast of Somalia.

Did anyone else use to think Alaska was an island? Totally argued with someone for an hour about it. Thank you, map of the US for making me feel dumb af!

 5/5 stupid rating

Every nation wanted to get their hands on the huge island with the perfectly straight side.

 Don't you wish you're girlfriend was grammatically correct like me?

 5/5 stupid rating

Don't you wish you proofread your Tweets?

Damn, seems like everyone havin a
birthday this year

♡ 5/5 stupid rating   💬   ⮀   ☆

*I will forgive this person if they were
born on February 29th.*

Every damn year we learn about the hollow cost in school, I'm tired of this shit!

♡ 5/5 stupid rating

I can see why they keep making you repeat the year.

 Where do I obtain a wedgie board? Do I have to make my own wedgie or can I buy one from a witch or vegan?

♡ 5/5 stupid rating

Just ask your nearest bully for a wedgie. They'll be happy to oblige.

My daughter just tried to tell me that
Plutonium doesn't come from Pluto.
At least she's pretty, huh?

♡ 5/5 stupid rating

*If beauty excuses stupidity,
you'd better be a supermodel.*

 I'm officially coma toast. the stress of
my job has killed me.

♡ 5/5 stupid rating

*What's worse than being toast and being
comatose? Being coma toast.*

Always been daddy's little angle …

♡ 5/5 stupid rating

You have an acute need of spelling lessons.

if theres a new jersey wheres the old one the US government is hiding too many secrets

♡ 5/5 stupid rating

They dragged it into the sea between England and France. Google 'Bergerac' to find out about the top-secret shit that went down there.

You take me for granite and one day
I'm not gonna put up with it anymore.

♡ 5/5 stupid rating   💬   ↻   ☆

At least they're treating you like an expensive
kitchen surface and not a cheap one.

Pear pressure is real

♡ 5/5 stupid rating

*No shit. My fruit bowl just made
me do meth.*

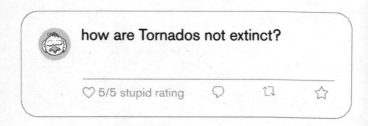

how are Tornados not extinct?

♡ 5/5 stupid rating

*Many tornados now live in sanctuaries,
where they're cared for by conservation
experts, and fed a regular diet
of Kansas farmhouses.*

i don't understand why they created multiple languages like what one wasn't good enough?

♡ 5/5 stupid rating

You know who created them, don't you?
Phrase book authors. The whole
thing is a scam.

20 billion people in the world trying to fit in, so imma try to stand outt

♡ 5/5 stupid rating

You're already standing out for inaccuracy.

I can't find any toast!!!
only bread!!

Same. Just found a loaf next to the toaster.
Guess I'll have to give up on my toast dream.

if both basketball teams just worked together they could score so many more points

♡ 5/5 stupid rating 〇 ⟲ ☆

Then everyone would be the champions forever and it would in no way undermine the entire point of sport.

A chicken seizure salad sounds good right now

♡ 5/5 stupid rating   💬   🔁   ☆

I only eat animals that have died of natural causes too.

someone should invent a place where you go to rent books. Like how blockbuster rented movies IMO

♡ 5/5 stupid rating   💬   ⮂   ☆

You'd be this dumb if you'd never been to a library.

 I never knew there were green apples??

♡ 5/5 stupid rating   💬   ⮂   ☆

Wait until they find out what colour oranges are.

I get to do my brother and his girlfriend's Maturity pictures today. So excited!

♡ 5/5 stupid rating   ☆

They'll be doing all the traditional maturity poses such as switching to lemonade after two drinks and not laughing at the word 'Uranus'.

I just drunk some inspired milk

♡ 5/5 stupid rating   ☆

What was it inspired to do?
Take up painting? Learn Spanish?
Now we'll never know.

Statistics show the teenage pregnancy rate drops significantly after the age of 20 …

♡ 5/5 stupid rating   💬   ↻   ☆

I'd say it drops to zero.

 Is the 4th July on the 15th or 16th?

♡ 5/5 stupid rating   💬   ↻   ☆

Think it might be on the 4th this year?

 Burned my chest trying to iron a wrinkle out of my shirt while wearing it.

♡ 5/5 stupid rating

Perhaps they were still dizzy from their spin in the washing machine.

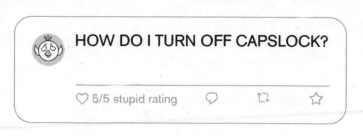

Okay, there's no need to shout about it.

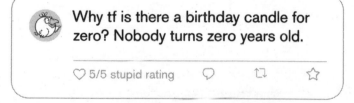

When you accidentally reveal you can't count past 9 yet.

How do islands not float away?

♡ 5/5 stupid rating

They're tied to the bottom of the ocean with strong ropes. Islanders have to be careful not to capsize them by putting all the heavy buildings on one side.

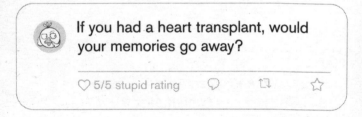

If you had a heart transplant, would your memories go away?

♡ 5/5 stupid rating

Yes, but you'd get some new ones. Because, as everyone knows, memories are stored in the heart.

I want a
life-size globe

Some people want the Earth.

So is like every country have a different moon or sumn' , cuz..

♡ 5/5 stupid rating   💬   ↺   ☆

Yes, that's why an extra one appears every time a country is accepted into the United Nations.

What does a quarter til four mean?
Like, why is it called that? Cause a
quarter is worth 25 cents, so why is it
15 minutes?

♡ 5/5 stupid rating

*If you had even a quarter of a brain, it would
be worth trying to explain.*

 This restaurant has got a great
umbeyonce

♡ 5/5 stupid rating

I've heard it's got a fantastic umrihanna too.

Somebody Tried To Tell Me There Was 50 States in America. Nuh Uh Cause The Scientists Found Out That Pluto Dont Exist. We Got 49 Dumbass

♡ 5/5 stupid rating   ☆

Plus, I think Delaware got reclassified as a dwarf state a few years back.

Been 18 for a year n half and never been to a clubbbb haha

♡ 5/5 stupid rating   ☆

I think you've been to the stupid club.
I suspect you've never left it, in fact.

Is it pronounced gif or gif?

♡ 5/5 stupid rating

Neither. It's pronounced gif.

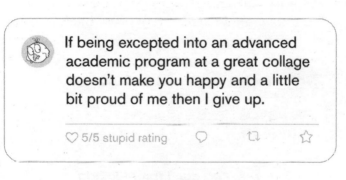

If being excepted into an advanced academic program at a great collage doesn't make you happy and a little bit proud of me then I give up.

♡ 5/5 stupid rating

I think they really made an exception in your case.

You speck French in London right?
Or is it British?

♡ 5/5 stupid rating   💬   ⇄   ☆

*They speck English, but not
properly like you.*

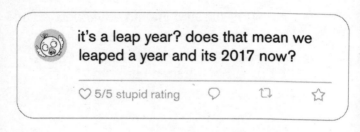

it's a leap year? does that mean we
leaped a year and its 2017 now?

♡ 5/5 stupid rating   💬   ⇄   ☆

*Yes, and don't forget to add
an extra year to your age too.*

Told my cousin he got me pregnant as an April fools joke. He was scared af LMAO

♡ 5/5 stupid rating

Er ... Why was he scared?

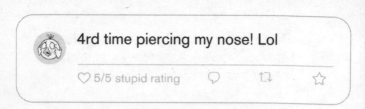

I'm only on my 3th.

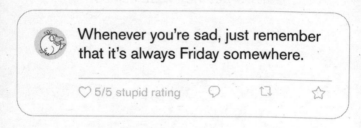

Not sure this checks out.

What's the name of the boat in the titanic?

♡ 5/5 stupid rating   ○   ⟲   ☆

Pretty sure the Carpathia makes an appearance too, so let's be nice and pretend that's what they were asking.

 MOCK MY WORDS "I WILL MAKE IT TO THE #BETAwards"

♡ 5/5 stupid rating   ○   ⟲   ☆

You know what? I'm not going to mock your words now you've asked me to.

We need more presidents like Lincoln, to bad Hitler assassinated him...

Wait, Hitler can travel through time?
Then we're all in trouble.

 I fucking love Pluto. I don't care that it is a moon or a dwarf star. I will always remember it as the planet named after mickey mouses' dog.

♡ 5/5 stupid rating   ♺   ☆

It was actually named after a god, so you've got the right letters in the wrong order.

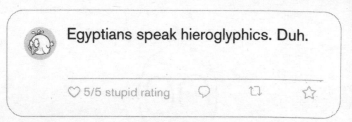

Egyptians speak hieroglyphics. Duh.

♡ 5/5 stupid rating   💬   ⇆   ☆

*I asked my Egyptian friend if this were true,
and he said, 'Eye, bird, feather, lion, snake'.*

WTF WHATS THE NUMBER FOR 911

♡ 5/5 stupid rating

Have you tried calling them to ask?

 If you claim to be a feminist and you're not vegan, then you're absolutely confused on what the meaning of feminist is.

♡ 5/5 stupid rating

If you claim to read this tweet and you're not absolutely confused, then you're absolutely confused on what the meaning of absolutely confused is.

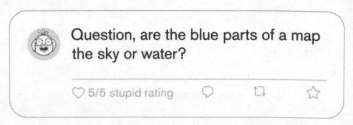

Question, are the blue parts of a map the sky or water?

♡ 5/5 stupid rating 　　💬　　⇄　　☆

They're the sky. The other bits have no sky above them, just an endless, unknowable void that melts the human brain.

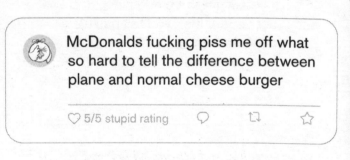

McDonalds fucking piss me off what so hard to tell the difference between plane and normal cheese burger

♡ 5/5 stupid rating 　　💬　　⇄　　☆

It's harder than you think. I ate half a 747 last night before I realized my mistake.

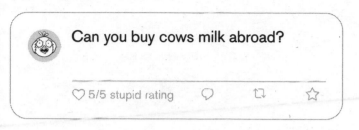

Can you buy cows milk abroad?

♡ 5/5 stupid rating   ○   ⇄   ☆

You might be able to find it in some larger supermarkets, but most countries prefer the zingy taste of cat milk.

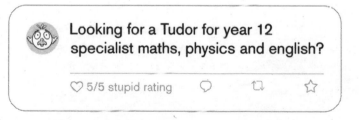

Looking for a Tudor for year 12 specialist maths, physics and english?

♡ 5/5 stupid rating   ○   ⇄   ☆

I'll see if Henry VII is free.

 Just found out my birthday is the same day as when I was born. Life is crazy aha.

♡ 5/5 stupid rating

You think that's crazy? My surname is the same as my second name.

Who was the first man to step on the sun?

♡ 5/5 stupid rating

No one will ever forget those famous words, 'One small step for man, one AAARRRRGGHHHH!'

If you don't know the difference between 'there', 'their' and 'they're', your an idiot.

♡ 5/5 stupid rating

An unfortunate mistake? Or an elaborate way of baiting grammar pedants?

Is it possible for tattoos to be passed on from parent to child???

♡ 5/5 stupid rating

I hope so, because otherwise the 666 I found on my head is rather worrying.

I asked her... babe, how much did you love me when we first met? She said 0. okay, what about now?... a billion times that.

♡ 5/5 stupid rating

I really hope she knows that zero times a billion is still zero, and this was a subtle burn.

Chess is all luck, no strategy. It all depends on what pieces you get.

I feel the same about cryptic crosswords. Some lucky people fill in letters at random and get them right.

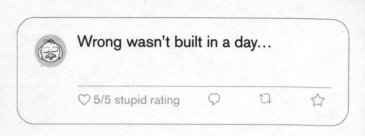

Wrong wasn't built in a day...

♡ 5/5 stupid rating

*I'm sensing that your wrong has been
built over a whole lifetime.*

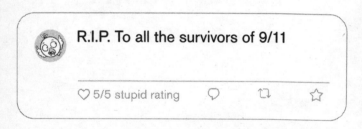

R.I.P. To all the survivors of 9/11

♡ 5/5 stupid rating

*Just because they're not dead, it doesn't
mean they can't rest in peace.*

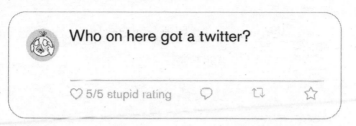

Who on here got a twitter?

♡ 5/5 stupid rating 💬 ↻ ☆

You're asking that on Twitter? Do you walk into bars and shout, 'Who here in a bar?'

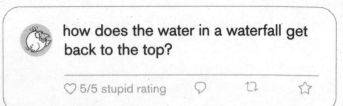

how does the water in a waterfall get back to the top?

♡ 5/5 stupid rating

Sadly, many of these great natural attractions can no longer afford full-time waterfall refillers. Please consider volunteering at your local one.

I wish I had an older twin brother who looked like me so I could use his I.D. to do adult things like go to the bar.

♡ 5/5 stupid rating

Yeah, because if he was born before midnight and you were born after it, you could get into bars a whole day earlier.

My sprit animal is a cantelope

♡ 5/5 stupid rating   ◯   ⇄   ☆

Mine is a watermelon.

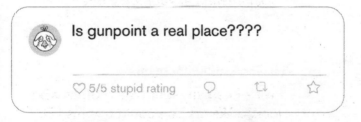

Is gunpoint a real place????

♡ 5/5 stupid rating   ◯   ⇄   ☆

Sure, the police hold criminals there before placing them under somewhere called 'Arrest'.

I'm ostrich-sized for believing in myself and being proud of what I am.

♡ 5/5 stupid rating   💬   ⟲   ☆

If being the size of a fully-grown ostrich is who you really are, don't let anyone exclude you.

 Having some filet minion

♡ 5/5 stupid rating   💬   ⟲   ☆

Not even Gru would be evil enough to grill and eat his little followers.

 Ain't had time to play on my phone because I work 24/7 5 days a week.

♡ 5/5 stupid rating

You work for 24 minutes an hour, 7 hours a day, 5 days a week? Sounds like you'll have plenty of time to play on your phone.

I'm so elittleret

♡ 5/5 stupid rating

To be fair, it was mean of them to make 'illiterate' quite hard to spell.

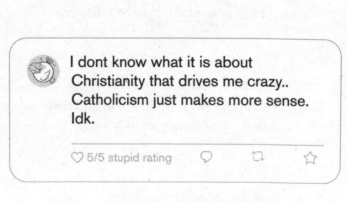

I dont know what it is about Christianity that drives me crazy.. Catholicism just makes more sense. Idk.

♡ 5/5 stupid rating

I'm currently a Muslim, but I'm thinking about converting to Islam.

I don't worry about the price of gas going up, I only ever put twenty dollars in at a time.

♡ 5/5 stupid rating

Big oil will probably offer you millions of dollars to hush this up. If everyone catches on to your system, they're finished.

 you know what bitch I'm just gonna say it; I don't believe in horses

♡ 5/5 stupid rating

I'm with you. All those big things running around fields are clearly just actors in pantomime costumes.

Is the same cloud covering the sun all over the world? #lifequestions

Yes, that cloud you can see covers the sun everywhere. Even places where it's currently night.

I bought my friend 4 pregnancy tests... they all came out positive & now she crying... she gon ask me "how tf am I going to afford to feed 4 kids"

♡ 5/5 stupid rating

You're not done yet. Keep testing until you get a negative one to find out how many children she'll have in total.

 Watching the Titanic, such a beautiful movie it always gets me. Makes me wanna go on a cruise like that one day:)

♡ 5/5 stupid rating

What, exactly like that?

 Did the world used to be black and white? I mean isn't that why the photos in history books are black and white?

♡ 5/5 stupid rating

That's correct. Colour was actually invented in the late nineteenth century, but most ordinary people had to wait a few years before they could afford to see in it.

Its crazy to me how babies can understand/speak other languages besides English. Like when a 1 y/o kids speak Spanish or creole or like a diff language lol

♡ 5/5 stupid rating   ↻   ☆

Does this person think English comes pre-installed on all babies like iOS, and they have to learn all the others?

 How did people in the Middle Ages know what skeletons look like without X-ray machines?

♡ 5/5 stupid rating   ↻   ☆

It's especially puzzling when you remember that no one ever died back then.

how the fuck the moon cover the sun if the sun is bigger?

♡ 5/5 stupid rating   ☆

*I can cover them both with my hand,
so they must both be pretty tiny.*

 dogs cant talk, so do they have brains? I know they walk but it's only because we are telling them to walk?

♡ 5/5 stupid rating   ☆

*I've heard that some things without
brains can even use Twitter.*

What goes around comes around.
Caramel is a bitch.

♡ 5/5 stupid rating   💬   ⇄   ☆

*You're telling me. I lost a filling
to some caramel fudge once.*

 Can't wait until I turn 21, I'll finally be
allowed to drink and drive.

♡ 5/5 stupid rating   💬   ⇄   ☆

*Arrest this guy for driving under
the influence of stupidity.*

Say what u like about Lance Armstrong… but being the first man to walk on the moon is an amazing achievement… they can't never take that away from him.

♡ 5/5 stupid rating

True. They can strip him of his titles, but he'll always have that moon stuff that happened before he was born.

 Death row inmates, what was your last meal?

♡ 5/5 stupid rating

Hello? Come on, answer the question. Honestly, some people are so rude.

how did beyonce go #1 in 100 countries when there's only 7? africa, europe, asia and i can't remember the rest

♡ 5/5 stupid rating   💬   ↻   ☆

This tweet's got you looking so crazy right now.

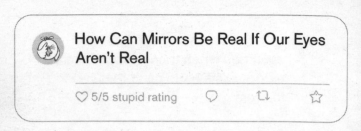

*They're not. If you move quick enough,
you'll catch them out.*

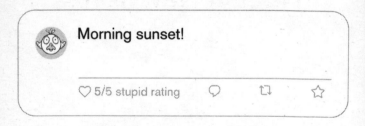

*You win the prize for dumbest
tweet in the fewest words.*

Goodbye America!
HELLO New York!

HELLO idiot!

 Soo I was thinking of baking cookies for everyone at work tomorrow, and I need to double the recipe to have enough, but if I double the temperature my oven wont set to 800.

♡ 5/5 stupid rating   ☆

Not sure if this person should be allowed to have an oven.

GUYS there's 4 lemon halves in my trash. He squeezed a whole lemon into my cup?

♡ 5/5 stupid rating

When life gives you lemons, magically cut them into four halves.

 Why can the police never figure out who the murderer was lmao like just ask the person who died is it really that hard???

♡ 5/5 stupid rating

Come on, police. Put those donuts down and get your Ouija boards out.

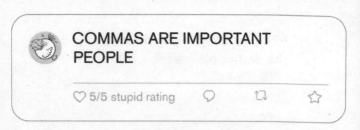

Without them, it might sound like you're claiming commas are people.

I don't know about you, but I'm not feeling very relaxed at all right now.

How do people drown lmao just drink the water lol

♡ 5/5 stupid rating   💬   ⇄   ☆

Warning: This method might not work if you're drowning in anything bigger than a glass.

 i don't understand why people always say that the mona lisa is Leonardo da vinci's best work. i really likes his role in Titanic.

♡ 5/5 stupid rating   💬   ⇄   ☆

I think he was best in Teenage Mutant Ninja Turtles.

Challenging black feminist outlook does not make you a massaginist! Ideas should bring us together not set us apart.

♡ 5/5 stupid rating ◯ ↺ ☆

I love massages. No one could call me a massaginist.

I have two sides… the nicest girl you'll ever meet… and twisted fucking cycle path…

♡ 5/5 stupid rating

Do you like slightly lengthening the journeys of cyclists? Then you might be a twisted fucking cycle path too.

 Tired of ppl telling me I can't spell lol like OK i know.. like what do you want me to do go back to the 3th grade or something?

♡ 5/5 stupid rating

I think you should go back to pre-school.

There's always a 50/50 chance it will rain. Either it will or it won't.

♡ 5/5 stupid rating ◯ ⇄ ☆

Vegas was built on people like this.

 If there is a new moon every month, where does the old one go?

♡ 5/5 stupid rating ◯ ⇄ ☆

A lot of people buy their moons second-hand. There's no shame in it.

If wings come from a bird, why is there buffalo wings? do buffalos have wings I am unaware of? someone please explain for me

♡ 5/5 stupid rating

Yes, Buffalo wings come from buffalos. Scientists have genetically modified them to sprout hundreds of chicken wings each. The food's name is nothing to with its origin in Buffalo, New York.

 If you use facial recognition for anything… the govt has your face lol

♡ 5/5 stupid rating

This person is going to freak when they find out about passports.

Why the hell did Benjamin Franklin have to invent lightning /:

He was trying to create a weapon that could take out his enemies. Then he lost control of it, and now look where we are.

Don't go Jason Waterfalls <3 that song

♡ 5/5 stupid rating

It's up there with 'Tony Danza' by Elton John and 'Sue Lawley' by The Police.

Life would be different if I was someone different tbh

♡ 5/5 stupid rating

So dumb it's deep.

Book readers are ever reading and never coming to true knowledge. Read books and you will be dumber after reading them because your mind is polluted by idiots that also read books only to write more books.

♡ 5/5 stupid rating

While it might not be true for all books, I hope this one has made you at least a little dumber.